ETERNAL MEXICO

The gnome-like spires of the Sierra de los Organos glow in the reflected light of a brilliant sunset. Rising abruptly from the plains of Zacatecas, this beautiful landscape has been the backdrop for numerous western films.

ETERNAL MEXICO

Photography and text by Robert Frerck

Foreword by José Iturriaga

CHRONICLE BOOKS

SAN FRANCISCO

For inquiries regarding prints or rights of reproduction for any of the images seen in *Eternal Mexico* please contact:

Odyssey Productions
2633 North Greenview
Chicago, Illinois 60614
Tel: 312 883 1965
Fax: 312 883 0929

Printed in Hong Kong.

ISBN 0-8118-1024-0

Book and cover design: Reuter Design, San Francisco

Library of Congress Cataloging-in-Publication Data available.

10 9 8 7 6 5 4 3 2 1

Distributed in Canada by Raincoast Books
8680 Cambie Street
Vancouver, BC V6P 6M9

Chronicle Books
275 Fifth Street
San Francisco, CA 94103

The snow on Popocatépetl's perfect crown catches the first sunlight of a winter's day, while the Church of the Remedies atop Cholula's Great Pyramid sits in shadow. The pyramid, one of the largest in Mesoamerica, was constructed over a period of 600 years.

CONTENTS

ACKNOWLEDGMENTS

I dedicate *Eternal Mexico* to

Itziar, Manuel, and Kerman Larrea:
My "family" in Mexico, for their endless patience and the sanctuary
their home provided during my many extended trips
and
Paulina and Pablo Ojeda:
To their new life together and all that they symbolize
for the future of their country.

My work in this book would not have been possible without the generous support of many friends on both sides of our common border. In particular, Juan Buendia, Rosalinda Rodriquez, Fernando Ruiz, Bernard Forat, Marco Cuevas, Eduardo Amezcua, and so many others past and present at the Secretaria de Turismo in Mexico City. Also a special thank you to my good friends: Felipe, Anna and Andres Siegel, and especially Marisa Siegel, who was always there with enthusiasm, encouragement, and help. And Señor Castro y Castro of the Fundacion Miguel Aleman, whose advice and guidance was always on the mark and greatly appreciated. Plus warm thanks to Katherine Pearse of Mexicana Airlines, Pedro Bosch, Stewart Cornew, Amy Bortz, and Sandra Saias of Edelman Worldwide, and the countless others who took the time, opened their homes, and shared their experiences with me.

Above all I owe the realization of this book to my very good friends Walter and Sara Van Enck for their support, and to Laurie, Jeff, Cecilia, and Connie, for hours of editing and the patience and hard work that allowed me the time to devote to Mexico. A special thanks to my brother Walter for sharing my travels through some of the wildest parts of Baja and northern Mexico. And finally to Frances, whose insights enrich many of my experiences, and who shares my love for Mexico's landscape, history, and people.

FOREWORD

BY JOSÉ N. ITURRIAGA

Since the sixteenth century, Mexico has been a focus of world attraction for many reasons. On the one hand, nature has bestowed on this country nearly all the possible landscapes and climates that exist on earth. On the other, the human element is remarkable for the variety of indigenous peoples, enriched by genes from elsewhere.

Indeed, Mexico combines tropical latitudes with high altitudes—some rising more than 18,500 feet above sea level—which results in everything from deserts with no apparent plant or animal life to unending snows; from beaches that are hot all year long to forests dense with a multitude of pines; from tropical jungles whose three levels of vegetation permanently obscure the sky to forests of enormous cactus; from small marine lakes where crocodiles proliferate to alpine lakes high in the mountains. The ethnic diversity of the Mexican people is no less astonishing: more than fifty-six distinct indigenous groups still exist in Mexico, each with its own autochthonous language; and those populations combined total more than ten million inhabitants. The natural and cultural richness of this nation is the principal appeal for the enormous number of foreign travelers who have visited Mexico over the last five centuries.

The number of visitors to Mexico is impossible to count, and the number of those who have also written about it runs in the thousands. In the sixteenth century, conquistadors and evangelizing monks predominated; in the following two centuries came inquiring priests, viceroys, other civil and military authorities, and a few scientists.

In 1821, Mexico gained its independence from Spain, which generated a huge stream of visitors eager to see the newborn country, which for three hundred years had been practically closed to foreigners. The influx of a great variety of travelers thus multiplied, and in the twentieth century, this flow increased, aided by advances in transportation.

The list of photographers who have visited Mexico, and who have attempted to capture it with their lenses and pens, begins with the Englishman Frederick Catherwood, who traveled throughout the Yucatán in 1839 armed with his daguerreotype. To this tradition belongs Robert Frerck, the author of this book, whose photographic images are illustrations not only for foreign eyes but also for Mexican eyes. Although it is said that an image speaks for itself, Frerck complements his visual voice with his own eloquent writings. Sensitively capturing the magic of Mexico, this book calls to mind the illuminating words of Pablo Neruda, Nobel prize–winning poet from Chile, who wrote in *Confieso Que He Vivido. Memorias:* "Mexico, flowering and thorny, dry and tempestuous, extremes of color and design, extremes of eruption and creation, I cover myself with its charm and unexpected light. . . . I wandered, I ran along all its coasts, its high steep coasts, burning with perpetual phosphoric lightning. I walked through all those splendid, mysterious syllables, those dawning sounds. Mexico, the last of the magical countries; the magic of antiquity and history, the magic of music and geography. . . . Nowhere in America, not even in all the planet, is there a country of more human depth than Mexico and its people."

MEXICO

Mexicali •
• Ensenada

Baja
California

• Pinacate

Cataviña •

Sonora

Chihuahua

Sierra Rica •
• Sierra del Carmen

Guaymas •

• Chihuahua

Basaseachic •   • Cuauhtémoc

Cueva Pintada •

Baja
California
Sur

• Cañon del Cobre

Coahuila

Loreto •

Los Mochis •

Gulf of
California

Sinaloa

• Monterrey

Durango

Nuevo
León

Gulf of Mexico

Durango •

La Paz •

Zacatecas

Real
de Catorce

San Lucas •

Mazatlán •

Sierra de los Organos •

Tamaulipas

Zacatecas •

San Luis
Potosí

Nayarit

Aguascalientes

• Tampico

Querétaro

• San Blas

Guanajuato •

Hidalgo

El Tajín •

Puerto Vallarta •

• Guadalajara

Guanajuato

• Tula

Pachuca

Bahía de
Campeche

Tizimín •
• Cancún

Mérida •
• Chichén Itzá

Yucatán
• Uxmal

Tulum •

Isla de
Cozumel

Jalisco

Pátzcuaro •

Mexico

Xalapa •

• Campeche

Quintana
Roo

Manzanillo •   • Colima

Michoacán

Mexico City ✪

Malinalco •

Tlaxcala

Cholula

• La Antigua

Veracruz

Hochob •

Chetumal •

Campeche

Morelos

Cuernavaca •

Puebla

Catemaco •

Tabasco

Pacific Ocean

Guerrero

Taxco •

Veracruz

Palenque •

Oaxaca

Tuxtla Gutiérrez •

• Acapulco

Oaxaca •

Monte Albán •

Chiapa de Corzo •

• San Cristóbal de las Casas

Chiapas

Golfo de
Tehuantepec

INTRODUCTION

BY ROBERT FRERCK

My personal exploration of Mexico began nearly thirty years ago when I was swept beneath majestic cliffs while rafting the surging waters of the Río Bravo (Rio Grande). Since then I have witnessed the night vigil of the Day of the Dead, probed the jungle shroud that envelopes the Maya pyramids of Yaxchilán, and swum in the crystalline waters in the shadow of Tulum.

I have traveled over one hundred thousand miles along Mexico's back roads, compelled to search out Mexico's hidden secrets. I have been rewarded by discovering truly magical places such as the nearly inaccessible *barrancas* of Baja California's Sierra de San Francisco; the Arroyo de San Pablo, a pristine Garden of Eden fed by tiny streams, its canyon walls awash with prehistoric rock art; and the theatrical, eroded rock formations and exotic flora of the Cataviña Boulderfield. On the mainland there is Basaseachic's elegant plume of water, cascading from such heights that it vaporizes before reaching the end of its long fall. I remember my campsite on the banks of the Usumacinta, where I listened to the screams of monkeys at dusk and awoke to find fresh puma tracks outside my tent.

My favorite experience occurred on a mountainside in Michoacán. Thousands of migrating Monarch butterflies enveloped me, covering my shoulders and clinging to my camera. Imagine the indescribable soft rustle of a million butterfly wings.

My most enduring memories, however, are of Mexico's people. They are open and generous with a tremendous vitality, a devotion to family, and a legendary resilience in the face of hardship. Even the most humble farmer stood with great dignity as I took his portrait. Pride shone through the eyes of the craftsman who showed me his replicas of Maya sculptures. With each piece he fashioned, he cemented a bond with the over one-thousand-year history of his people.

It is my hope that this book does justice to the eternal beauty of Mexico and to the Mexican people, who express their pride in the beauty of their structures, arts, and relationships as naturally as they breathe.

Robert Frerck

Xochimilco, southeast of Mexico City, is a remnant of once-vast lakes on which the Aztecs built their capital of Tenochtitlán. These "floating gardens" were created in the thirteenth century by the Chinampaneca Indians as rafts for farming flowers and vegetables. After hundreds of years, the rafts rooted to the shallow lake bed and formed islands called chinampas. Produce is transported not by trucks, but by boats via a labyrinth of canals. Today two areas remain; one is a popular Sunday destination for families

escaping the crowds of Mexico City, where for a few hours they can hire a flower bedecked trajinera *and glide across the waters to the serenades of passing mariachi bands.*

The other is an ecological reserve where a visitor can experience the ambience of the central valley of Mexico as it might have been in the time of the Aztecs.

The Algodones Dunes straddle the United States-Mexico border east of Mexicali in the state of Baja California, one of the driest areas of North America. The 254-square-mile dunes were formed along the edge of an extinct sea during the Pleistocene period.

This luxuriant fern jungle covers a hillside near Xalapa, Veracruz. An ever-present mist called chipichipi *shrouds these valleys between the coastal plains and central highlands.*

Coffee, mango, bananas, and orchids from the tropical lowlands share this lush environment with pears and apples common to the higher temperate zone.

Equal to the density of the fern jungle are the exuberant decorations found at Santa María Tonantzintla, where every inch of the domes and arches is covered with a syncretic pantheon of Christian saints, native fertility gods, and feathered warriors. Fashioned by Indian craftsmen, its folk beauty portrays a richness in heaven that was denied them on earth.

The Maya temple at Hochob is glimpsed through Campeche's thick underbrush. The deep relief of the facade portrays the gigantic face of Chac, the Maya rain god. To enter, one must pass into the fierce mouth, its lips curled back, revealing rows of now-broken incisors. Above the door two eyes gaze unblinking through the centuries. The Maya considered the secret chambers within the pyramids and temples to be sacred entryways into the underworld.

The turquoise waters of Agua Azul spill over limestone steps in a ribbon of cascades and series of tranquil pools that stretches for miles through the jungles of northern Chiapas.

The world's tallest cactus, the giant cardon, pierces the sky of the wind-eroded landscape of the Cataviña Boulderfield. Baja California's most spectacular desert scenery culminates

here in the peninsula's largest national park, the Parque Natural del Desierto Central.

A rustic cabaña *provides a sheltered vista of the pure white sands of Quintana Roo's Caribbean coastline south of Tulum. This stretch of magnificent beach remains a paradise far removed from the bustle of Cancún's tourist hotels and discos.*

Rows of maguey spread to the horizon near Tequila west of Guadalajara. Tequila, mezcal, and pulque are all alcoholic beverages traditionally distilled from various maguey agave plants. Pre-Hispanic peoples considered pulque a gift from the gods reserved for use by the nobility; imbibing by commoners was punishable by death.

Early morning mist softens the shoreline of a small lake near San Miguel de Allende, where horses and burros graze oblivious to their serene surroundings.

Modeled in stone and stucco, this six-and-a-half-foot-tall image of the Maya sun god flanks the staircase of a pyramid at Kohunlich in southern Quintana Roo.

YUCATÁN PENÍNSULA

CAMPECHE, QUINTANA ROO, AND YUCATÁN

The Yucatán Peninsula is a vast limestone-and-coral shelf of approximately 44,000 square miles projecting into the Gulf of Mexico. Extremely porous, the soil absorbs rainwater before it can collect on the surface; consequently, what water is available is found in underground rivers and natural sink-holes called cenotes. It was around these life-supporting cenotes that the great Maya cities developed. As Maya mythology and religion evolved, great religious significance was attached to these sources of water. The sacred cenote of Chichén Itzá, for example, gave the city its name, which means "at the mouth of the well of the Itzá." When explored it offered up thousands of valuable jade and gold artifacts as well as the remains of human sacrificial victims.

Although cenotes are the most distinctive feature of the peninsula's landscape, its 992 miles of coastline feature some of the world's most glorious beaches. The finest lie along the eastern Caribbean shore where coral reefs provide protected inlets and produce shorelines with soft, white sand. It was along this eastern Yucatán coast that the Spanish sailed in 1517 and where the epoch-making clashes between the forces of the New and Old Worlds first occurred.

The lovely white beaches of Quintana Roo's Caribbean coast draw hundreds of thousands of visitors annually. Ninety-three miles south of the mega-resort of Cancún, the beaches retain their peaceful, unhurried feeling much as they were in 1518 when the Spaniard Juan de Grijalva sailed this coast. Although Spanish ships had first touched the Mexican mainland the year before, they had turned west into the Gulf of Mexico instead of heading south. Three days out of Cuba, Grijalva's four small vessels first sighted the island

of Cozumel. After rounding its southern cape, he passed close enough to the mainland to see ceremonial fires burning in the watchtowers and temples of Tulum, the Maya

"City of the Dawn" perched on cliffs above the azure water.

"**T**here is no rudeness or barbarity in the design or proportions; on the contrary, the whole wears an air of architectural symmetry and grandeur." With these words, the American explorer John Lloyd Stephens conveyed his impression of the Palace of the Governor at Uxmal in 1840. One hundred and fifty years later, anyone fortunate enough to witness the sun's first warm rays caressing the elegant building can only affirm Stephens's description. At least 20,000 hand-carved stones are fitted together in the 328-foot

facade that twentieth-century archaeologist Sylvanus Morley called "the most magnificent, the most spectacular single building in all pre-Columbian history and art." Unlike other buildings at Uxmal, the palace was constructed facing southeast—which would have allowed a Maya astronomer to stand in the central doorway and sight directly over a pyramid three miles distant to the point on the horizon where Venus rises as the morning star.

An immense terraced platform elevates the Palace of the Governor above the flat landscape of the Yucatán. Beyond and slightly higher is the steeply staired, 128-foot Pyramid

of the Magician, while to the left are the House of the Turtles and the four temples of the Nunnery Quadrangle. Uxmal was settled about A.D. 600, and its great structures

were built over the next three centuries in what has become known as the Puuc style. Typically its plain lower surfaces contrast with an upper band of rich texture often

containing stylized images of Chac. The long-nosed image of Chac appears everywhere, a constant reminder that in a land where water was scarce, the god of rain was all important. For reasons that remain a mystery, the city was deserted by A.D. *900, although there is speculation that Chac failed his people and years of drought forced them to flee.*

Seventeen miles from Uxmal on what has become known as the Puuc Route, named for the numerous nearby archaeological sites built in that architectural style, are the ruins of Sayil. At its peak, 10,000 people lived in Sayil. Its most impressive structure was the one hundred-room Great Palace. A grand stairway splits the façade and leads up through three terraces supported by columns and embellished with huge Chac masks and descending gods. The palace was a royal residence for 150 years before Sayil was abandoned

in approximately A.D. 900. Local legend has it, however, that possibly not all the residents have departed; it is believed that the palace is haunted, a notion supported by reports that on Good Friday music is heard echoing through the ruins.

A reclining Chac Mool stares toward the setting sun, his hands cradling a ceremonial disk that may have once held the hearts of sacrificial victims. The grim-faced god is framed by columns capped with scaled tails reaching upward for a roof that no longer exists, their bases the gaping, fanged mouths of snakes. These columns on the Temple of the Warriors at Chichén Itzá represent Kukulcán, the Maya version of the feathered serpent Quetzalcóatl. Chichén Itzá reached its apotheosis in the ninth through thirteenth centuries, yet its story remains enigmatic to archaeologists. Its architecture is of two distinct phases, suggesting a mix of cultural influences. The refinement of the Maya's earlier buildings was replaced with a harsher, more imposing style reminiscent of the Toltecs of central Mexico. Some scholars have suggested an invasion by the Toltecs is responsible for the changes in style, while others think the opposite, that Tula, the Toltec capital, might have been an outpost of Chichén Itzá.

The Caracol is one of Chichén Itzá's most fascinating structures. Thought to have served as an observatory for astronomical calculations, it is a graceful circular building embellished with Chac masks. Beyond the Caracol the great Pyramid of Kukulcán rises.

This small pool next to Cenote Azul is located near Akumal on the Quintana Roo coast. Surrounded by mangroves and palms, its shady solitude is a treat for the infrequent visitor.

To the east of Chichén Itzá, at Dzitnup near Valladolid, lies this cenote where local children prepare for a dip in its crystal-clear waters. Draped in stalactites and with only a tiny aperture open to the sky, Dzitnup is both cavern and cenote, and in ancient times would have been approached with awe. Sacred features of the landscape, caves were considered transitions from the physical world to the spirit world, entrances into the dreaded Maya underworld, a realm of unending darkness.

Statues of four beautiful women contemplate now-vacant fields that centuries ago bustled with activity. The elegance of the structure upon which they perch hints at the vanished wealth of the Yaxcopoil Hacienda. Beginning in 1875, a worldwide demand for twine and rope made from the fibers of the henequén plant spawned the sisal industry, and with it, vast fortunes for owners of the plantations surrounding Mérida. Although built in the seventeenth century, it was in the boom years of henequén cultivation that Yaxcopoil grew into

one of the Yucatán's most important rural estates, counting 22,000 cultivated acres. Many of the entrepreneurs who built these lavish mansions were members of the social elite in

Mérida, for a short time making it one of the world's wealthiest cities. As quickly as these great riches were amassed, though, they dissipated. The Revolution of 1910 and the

agrarian reforms that followed caused the breakup of the great haciendas. Today, crumbling ruins scattered across northern Yucatán are the only reminders of this era of prosperity.

Every 6 January, thousands of pilgrims from across the Yucatán flock to the town of Tizimín, north of Valladolid, to celebrate the Day of the Three Kings. Like many Mexican festivals, the Day of the Three Kings fuses religious piety and popular entertainment. A seemingly endless line of the devout passes through the ancient monastery to be blessed by the santos, *while outside a lively market provides a colorful diversion.*

At the center of the bustling market, this young man has trained his pet canary and parakeet to tell fortunes by selecting a slip of paper with their beaks. For a few centavos, *customers receive advice on matters of health, employment, and, of course, love; possibly even a lucky national lottery number.*

All is a blur as a Maya girl circles rapidly on her carousel mount. Amusement rides, bullfights, fireworks, traditional dance performances, and endless food, noise, and color are all part of the excitement to be found in Tizimín during the holiday.

Three young vaqueros *pose on horseback as their parents proudly shout encouragement from the sidelines. Traveling photographers, equipped with a variety of props and handpainted backdrops, are common at local festivals. The bright background shown here shouts out for remembrance of Tizimín and its Three Kings celebration.*

*T*his ten-foot stone head was found at San Lorenzo in southern Veracruz. San Lorenzo was the first great Olmec ceremonial center in a civilization that flourished from 1500 B.C. to 100 B.C. Olmec influence was so widespread that it is considered the mother culture of Mesoamerica. These huge heads, some weighing up to thirty tons, were transported thirty-seven miles from their quarry to San Lorenzo.

GULF COAST

TABASCO AND VERACRUZ

Few areas of Mexico boast as exotic a mixture of terrain as the Gulf Coast. It stretches from the steamy jungles of Tabasco into the rolling foothills of Veracruz and culminates in the grandeur of the sierra at Pico de Orizaba, the country's highest mountain.

The history of the region parallels the richness of its landscapes. The humid lowlands were the incubator of America's earliest civilization. Here, 3,000 years ago, the Olmecs raised the first pyramid, the defining symbol of Mesoamerican culture.

Twenty-five hundred years later, near present-day Veracruz, the Spanish made their initial contact with the coastal Indians and the envoys of the Aztec empire. Eventually, Veracruz became Mexico's gateway to the world. Rulers, rebels, and incomparable riches passed through its port, making Veracruz second only to Mexico City in importance. Today, oil, agricultural products, and manufactured goods have replaced silver as the area's top exports.

The mysterious Pyramid of the Niches towers above the surrounding structures of El Tajín. This most important center of classic Veracruz culture reached its peak between the ninth and eleventh centuries. Little is known about the purpose of the Pyramid. Because it aligns with the points of the compass and contains a total of 365 niches, it is believed to have functioned as an astronomical calendar.

Roots of ancient trees surround and support the remaining walls of what is locally referred to as the House of Cortés in La Antigua. Founded by Hernán Cortés in 1519, and originally called Villa Rica de la Vera Cruz, it is believed to have been here that the explorer scuttled his ships to discourage retreat.

On Good Friday, 21 April 1519, Cortés dropped anchor here and the following day made his first contact with Moctezuma's envoys. As a protective measure, the Spaniards constructed the first fortifications of San Juan de Ulúa as early as 1528, although it was not until 1598 that the city of Veracruz was officially established. Since then, Veracruz has remained Mexico's most important port and San Juan de Ulúa its principal (albeit not always successful) point of defense.

A *small roadside chapel, surrounded by sugarcane, contains a statue of a saint or* santo *and several perpetually lit candles in honor of a loved one killed at this site. During the observation of Dia de Muertos, shrines similar to this throughout the country are decorated with flowers and special offerings.*

Pico de Orizaba rises majestically above surrounding valleys and tiny Indian villages. Its eastern slopes fall into Veracruz while its western slopes lie in the state of Puebla. At 18,700 feet, Orizaba is the highest peak in Mexico and the third highest in North America. Its Aztec name is Citlaltépetl meaning "Star Mountain"—possibly because its snowy cap acted as a beacon that could be seen from miles away on starry nights.

Fishing nets are staked to the shallow bed of Lake Catemaco in southern Veracruz. Surrounded by volcanic cones and rolling green fields, this ten-mile-long lake is a favorite holiday retreat for Mexican families. Catemaco is also renowned for its traditions of herbal healing. A nearby mountaintop is reputed to be the site of an annual gathering of brujos (witch doctors) from around the world.

At daybreak, fishermen pull together to draw in their nets from the waters of Lake Catemaco, hoping to find a catch of mojarra *(perch) or* tegogolo, *a lake snail said to be an aphrodisiac and best eaten with chili and lime.*

Once the sun is up, it is time for drying and repairing nets stretched along the waterfront.

Wild bougainvillaea drapes banana trees and coffee plants on a plantation near Xalapa.

Near Papantla in northern Veracruz, two women draw water from a stream.

The tile wall of a colonial home provides a vibrant backdrop to a fruit vendor in Coatepec, just south of Xalapa.

A *plumed headdress with a jester god, the sign of kings mounted on the front, is passed by Maya ruler Pacal to his son Kan-Xul as he is about to ascend the throne of Palenque. Kan-Xul leans forward expectantly to receive his crown, the first part of the regalia that will transform him into a king. Under his family's benevolent rule, the city reached its zenith in the seventh and eighth centuries. Pacal himself lived over eighty years and directed the construction of much of the city's superlative architecture.*

SOUTHERN MEXICO

CHIAPAS AND OAXACA

The states of Oaxaca and Chiapas in southern Mexico contain some of the country's most varied and spectacular landscapes. This region is framed by the rugged Sierra Madre del Sur along its southern and western rims and the Chiapas highlands to the east. The Sierra Volcánica on the north is home to many of Mexico's most imposing volcanic peaks, and separates the area from central Mexico. A second geographic division occurs at the Isthmus of Tehuantepec, the narrowest part of Mexico and the real demarcation between North and Central America.

In the past, volcanoes, mountains, and the swamps and jungles of the isthmus combined to isolate large sections of the south not only from each other but from mainstream Mexican life as well. This has allowed the area to retain much of its traditional Indian and colonial culture, especially in the villages surrounding the cities of Oaxaca and San Cristóbal de las Casas. This is particularly true in the highlands of Chiapas, where descendants of the Maya continue to lead lives strongly similar to those of their historic brethren. Unfortunately this geographic isolation has also severely limited southern Mexico's economic growth, making it one of the poorest areas in the country. Today a lack of arable land and low employment are continuing conditions.

Emerald jungles spill around Palenque's cream-colored stones, warming with the dawn. Sited on a narrow mountain shelf overlooking the coastal plains of neighboring Tabasco,

Palenque is considered by many to be the most beautiful of Maya ceremonial centers. To the right is the Palace, its four-story tower once used by priests for astronomical

observations. To the left is the terraced Temple of the Inscriptions, the tallest and most prominent of Palenque's structures. Deep within its mass of stone lies Pacal's royal tomb,

hidden for over twelve centuries until its discovery in 1952. Reached by descending a steep staircase, the burial chamber, its walls stuccoed with images of the nine lords of the

underworld, once contained Pacal's bejeweled skeleton and jade death mask.

Maya civilization reached its peak during the Classic period, approximately A.D. 200-900. Shortly thereafter, it came to a precipitous end and many of the great city-states—including Palenque, Uxmal, Yaxchilán, and Tikal—were abandoned for reasons that remain unclear. Consequently, power shifted to coastal Yucatán and the highlands of Chiapas and Guatemala. Today many mountain settlements are home to direct descendants of the Maya, who live and worship in ways that are similar to that of their forebears. In the Tzotzil village of Zinacantán, seven miles from the colonial city of San Cristóbal de las Casas, a mother and child dress in traditional Tzotzil outfits.

A *young Tzotzil woman, wearing a hand-embroidered* huipil, *uses a back-strap loom in the courtyard of her home in Zinacantán. Every village in the Chiapas highlands has its own distinctive style of dress, and weaving remains a living folk art, with strong social and religious associations. Local cooperatives aid weavers in selling their goods and encourage the revival of lost techniques and designs.*

Traditional garb is visible everywhere during the fiesta of San Sebastián, Zinacantán's major winter celebration. Sebastián, a martyr whose body was pierced by Roman arrows, was one of the first Christian saints introduced to the Zinacantecs. Before the conquest, Maya prisoners of war were executed by archers; hence San Sebastián found acceptance with the Zinacantecs, who believed that as a Spanish soldier he was pursued by the enemy Lacandon Indians and slain in a similar fashion.

The festival of San Sebastián is an important date on the sacred calendar of cyclical renewal that shapes the Zinacantec world-view. Zinacantán's religious leaders assume a responsibility (cargo) to serve the saint and their community for one year, and by performing prescribed ceremonies maintain cosmic order and carry the world forward through its cycle. On San Sebastián's day the cargo is accepted by the incoming alféreces and capitanes and a new cycle begins. At their feet lie bottles of posh, a potent home brew served on ceremonial occasions.

The steady rhythm of music is heard throughout the fiesta and plays an integral part of the ritual duties in the year ahead. The beribboned hats that are so characteristic of traditional Zinacantec dress resemble the elaborate feathered headdresses of the ancient Maya.

Four capitanes, *resplendent in elegant cloaks and peacock-feathered hats, are accompanied by musicians and a circle of* alféreces *as they lead a somber ceremonial dance, their rattles keeping time with the slow shuffle of feet. The religious leaders fast and forego sleep for the four days of the festival; this and the drinking of* posh *combine to induce a trance-like state.*

The Dance of the Animals abounds in pre-Columbian symbolism. Here, jaguar dancers wearing baggy spotted suits and tall hats perform next to negritos. The stuffed animals that they hold represent companion spirits, for it is believed that every person goes through life sharing his or her soul with an animal. Anything that happens to one being happens to the other; the death of an animal can result in its human companion falling ill or suffering "soul loss," a condition that can only be remedied by the intercession of a shaman.

Each troupe of dancers assumes the roles of supernatural entities, both good and evil. The jaguar acts as an intermediary between the world of the living and the world of the dead, while mossmen, draped from head to toe in Spanish moss, allude to Moss Mountain, the most sacred site in the highlands and the home of the mythical Earthlord.

These dancers are called pájaros (ravens) and are a manifestation of K'uk'ulchan (in Tzotzil), also known as Quetzalcóatl, the god of the ancient Toltecs. Represented with an ear of corn held in its beak, Quetzalcóatl is honored as the deity that first brought the grain to the Zinacantecs.

Clowns run through the crowds chased by a torito—a wooden "bull" covered in hide and aflame with flares. Skyrockets arching across the sky announce the start of each of the festival's many events. The celebration of San Sebastián is many things: a solemn religious event, a raucous living theater, and a morality play. It also commemorates the Zinacantec's ultimate victory over the Spanish conquistadores by demonstrating that the age-old customs of the Maya are still alive.

Fog clings tightly to a mountaintop where a Golgotha of tall wooden crosses rises above the Chamulan cemetery at Romerio. At the center of the ancient Maya universe was a giant ceiba tree—its roots were said to penetrate the underworld, while its trunk, with two branches forming a cross, reached into the heavens.

Wrapped in brightly colored sarapes, dancers surge through the narrow streets shaking tin or gourd maracas, *creating an ambience of riotous exuberance.*

While the fiesta of San Sebastián is celebrated in Zinacantán it is also observed in a very different way, forty-three miles to the west in Chiapa de Corzo. The Chiapanecs were historic enemies of the Zinacantecs, and here the men and boys wear striking costumes with carved wooden masks and blond wigs made of ixtle fiber, representing Spanish conquistadores.

San Sebastián's day is in fact just one event in the thirteen days of festivities collectively called the Fiesta de Enero. The men and boys in curious costumes are called parachicos. The drama stems from the story of a sickly young boy whose mother amused him with maracas shaken by her servants. Today it is entertainment for everyone.

The piety of the Fiesta de Enero, embodied by processions of the saints and accompanied by young girls carrying painted gourds with offerings, cannot escape the lightheartedness of the fiesta when drenched in confetti.

Between the Sierra Madre de Chiapas and the Chiapas highlands the Grijalva River flows. For twenty-two miles the river cuts a tortuous path through the mountains, leaving near-vertical cliffs that tower up to 3,900 feet above the water. Visitors can now take small boats through Sumidero Canyon, which flooded after the completion of the Chicoasén Dam in 1981, to experience one of Mexico's most awesome landscapes.

High on a mountaintop leveled by human hands sits Mexico's fabled ceremonial center, constructed over 2,000 years ago. The Mixtec called Monte Albán Sahandevui ("at the foot of heaven"), and at sunrise or sunset the site seems infused with a cosmic silence, a pivot point in the balance of celestial bodies. First occupied between 800 and 400 B.C.,

it underwent several successive building phases, culminating circa A.D. *250 and 750 when 25,000 people inhabited the surrounding slopes. Possibly owing to overexploitation of resources, Monte Albán was abandoned around* A.D. *800.*

Approximately at the start of the Christian era, the Zapotecs moved into the central valley and occupied Monte Albán. Their descendants still live in the surrounding villages, every Sunday attending the busy market at Tlacolula, south of Oaxaca City, to sell their produce and crafts. Here a young mother keeps both hands free for shopping by carrying her child in a bright rebozo.

Five little girls are dwarfed by the immense trunk of El Tule, the huge ahuehuete tree that stands between Tlacolula and Oaxaca. A type of cypress, El Tule measures 138 feet around and is believed to have the largest girth of any tree in the world. The giant has been growing for over 2,000 years, which makes it not only one of the largest, but one of the oldest living trees on the planet.

*S*everal hundred years after the decline of Monte Albán, a second great city rose to power at Mitla, twenty-five miles to the south. The Zapotecs erected one of their most exquisite

palaces here. The Hall of the Columns is distinguished by the six massive piers that once supported its roof. The structure is also famous for the intricate mosaics that grace the

exterior walls and a small interior patio. Each of the estimated 100,000 pieces of stone was hand-cut to fit complex geometric patterns of symbolic significance.

A *long colonnade leads the eye through the roofless interior of the great monastery at Cuilapan. Built in 1555, it is one of a number of monasteries established by the Dominicans in the central valley of Oaxaca. Cortés appreciated the rich fertility of this area and his influence is reflected in much of the early colonial history of the valley. Eventually he was awarded large haciendas here and was given the title of Marqués del Valle de Oaxaca.*

Gilding and polychrome ornamentation covers every surface of Santo Domingo, one of the most splendid interiors in Mexico. Construction of the church began in 1570 and was completed one hundred years later by artisans brought from Puebla and other distant cities. The elaborate carvings on the entry ceiling detail the extensive family tree of San Domingo de Guzmán, the Spanish monk who founded the Dominican order in the thirteenth century with strict vows of poverty, chastity, and obedience. The Dominicans

assumed the role of benefactors to the Indians, protecting them from exploitation, and, by adopting many of their local customs, made their conversion to a Christian God more acceptable to the Indians.

CENTRAL MEXICO

AGUASCALIENTES, GUANAJUATO, GUERRERO, HIDALGO, MEXICO, MICHOACÁN, MORELOS, PUEBLA, QUERÉTARO, SAN LUIS POTOSÍ, TLAXCALA, AND ZACATECAS

Bounded on the east by the Sierra Madre Oriental (an extension of the Rocky Mountains in the U.S.) and on the west by the Sierra Madre Occidental (an extension of the Sierra Nevada range), Central Mexico is a high plateau of rolling hills and towering, snow-capped volcanoes. The three great pre-Hispanic empires of Teotihuacán, the Toltecs, and the Aztecs all sprang forth from this land to dominate Mesoamerica. When the Spanish crossed the eastern sierra they must have felt quite at home, for these vast, dry plains strongly resemble the high *meseta* they had left behind in Castile and Extremadura. Indeed, cities they built here strongly resemble those of Cáceres and Salamanca.

The central valley was the setting for one of history's epochal events when on 8 November 1519 Cortés and his small army met the Aztec king Moctezuma, and forever changed the courses of both the New and Old Worlds.

Many things had drawn the Spanish to explore the New World. However, since they bore much of the expense of their expeditions themselves, recouping their investment with land, slaves, or mineral wealth was one of their primary concerns. Moctezuma unwittingly lured them on when he attempted to bribe them with gold to leave his country. This was a costly mistake, for it hardened the resolve of the Spanish in their plans for conquest. After the collapse of the Aztec civilization the Spanish scoured the countryside looking for the Indian mines. They found little gold, but in 1548 they struck silver in unimaginable amounts. The first mother lode was discovered in Zacatecas, followed within six

years by other fabulous strikes in Guanajuato and at Real del Monte near Pachuca.

In addition to being the geographic and historic center of the country, central Mexico is also the emotional heartland for the Mexican people. The area is Mexico's "melting pot" where the greatest mix of indigenous and European cultures has occurred. It is where haciendas and mines forged the nation's economy and where independence was first demanded and finally won. Mexico's economy and society has always been strongly centralized and even today, influence and power is directly correlated to one's distance from the capital.

Four massive stone figures dominate the countryside surrounding Tula, an ancient city cloaked in mystery and debate, sixty-two miles northwest of Mexico City. When Tula reigned supreme over central Mexico, these giant columns supported the roof of a temple that crowned the city's principal pyramid. It is believed that Tula was founded by nomadic northern tribes who settled here in the mid-tenth century and became known as the Toltecs. The ascendancy of Tula was short-lived, however; by the beginning of the twelfth century the site was vacant.

After the demise of Tula, power in central Mexico was contested by various groups, until the Aztecs finally achieved dominion in the early fifteenth century. Carved into living rock by the Aztecs, Malinalco is unique among Mesoamerican temples. Its location on a steeply terraced hillside commands spectacular views over the fertile Chalma Valley; however, it is the temple's interior that is truly extraordinary.

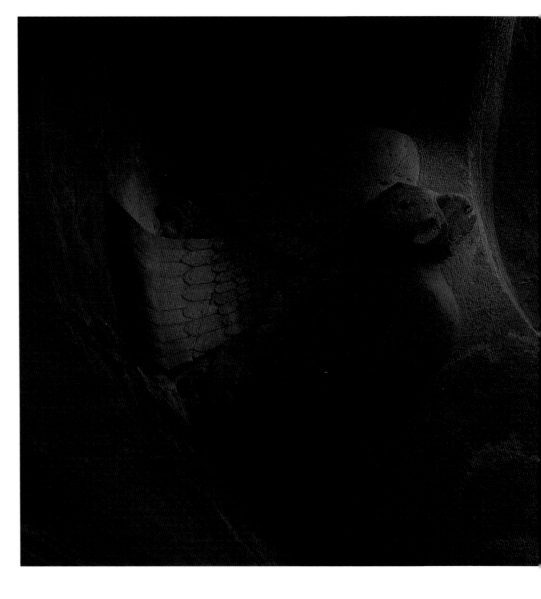

Entered through a deep cut, Malinalco was conceived as an architectural cave, completely hewn out of solid rock. A semicircular bench is edged with sculptured eagles and jaguars, symbols of the two great Aztec warrior cults. A third eagle faces the doorway; behind it, a small basin recessed into the floor received blood offerings. Ultimately they were to no avail; Huitzilopochtli, the Aztec god of war, was unable to protect the kingdom against a new invader, Cortés.

With the discovery of silver, dreams of fantastic wealth spurred prospectors to probe every corner of Mexico for new riches. In the mid-eighteenth century their efforts were rewarded in the rugged mountains of the Sierra Madre Oriental. For a time the mines of Real de Catorce were the country's third largest producers of silver and the city boasted a

population of 40,000. Today it's virtually a ghost town, only coming alive when the Huichol Indians make their annual pilgrimage from Nayarit to hold their peyote rituals during the fiesta of San Francisco.

Four years after the first great silver strike in 1548, muleteers discovered veins of silver in a steep hillside called Cuanax-huato *(Frog Hill)* by the Tarascan Indians. It took six years to reach the mother lode, which was to become La Valenciana, the world's richest silver mine. Over the next two centuries up to forty percent of the world's silver came out of these mines, which are still visible on the slopes beyond the domes of Guanajuato's colonial churches.

Angels hover in permanent suspension above a gold-encrusted altar in Guanajuato's La Valenciana church, built by the owner of the La Valenciana mine. The Conde de Rul was reputed to be the wealthiest man in Mexico, as he grandly demonstrated by footing the bill for this church—although it is hinted that he may have been trying to publicly atone for exploiting his miners.

Guanajuato's major mines—La Valenciana, Cata, and Minas de Rayas—featured great churches for the use of the miners and their families. This detail shows the Virgin of Guadalupe on the facade of the Cata church. The interior walls are covered with retablos, small paintings on tin painted by or for the miners, that depict stories of prayers, miracles, and faith.

In contrast to the rich textures of La Valenciana is this simple but charming element from the baroque facade of Santa María de Tonantzintla, near Puebla.

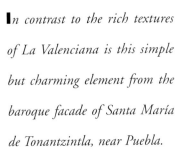

The first of Mexico's fabulous silver strikes occurred at Zacatecas in 1548, generating such wealth that the city grew to become second only to Mexico City in population. The affluent silver barons spared no expense when it came to the city's cathedral. Completed after 140 years of construction, the building is considered one of the finest examples of Hispanic-American architecture. This view of the principal facade shows a swirl of carved acanthus leaves, garlands, heavenly musicians, cherubs, and the Apostles, delicately preserved in pink stone.

Santos and oil paintings crowd a corner of the Felipe Siegel shop in Mexico City, a vignette of the rich artistic legacy of Mexico's colonial period. Originally, many of these pieces graced the small chapels of the great haciendas and private residences.

Here the sun and moon combine to shine down from the cathedral door. Visual treasures abound in Zacatecas, making this elegant city a favorite for aficionados of Mexican colonial architecture.

The dramatic Holy Week observances in Taxco are world-renowned for the pious devotion shown by their participants. For hours, long columns of hooded penitents shuffle slowly along, bearing their burdens. Some carry heavy crosses, others bundles of thorn brush tied to their shoulders, while some lash themselves with whips, in emulation of the pain and sacrifice of Christ.

Even before the mother lodes were tapped in Zacatecas and Guanajuato, silver had been discovered in Taxco, but it was not until 1743 that José de la Borda stumbled upon the richest vein. The fortune that he made beautified Taxco with mansions, gardens, and the cathedral of Santa Prisca, a masterpiece of baroque architecture. Historians speculate that the Conde de Rul built his church of La Valenciana in Guanajuato in an attempt to surpass his rival's efforts in Taxco.

*A*t twilight the twin towers of Santa Prisca cathedral rise above a solemn procession as it threads its way through the narrow cobblestone streets of Taxco.

*T*hroughout the night the faithful file through the city, testimony that Mexico remains one of the world's most devoutly Catholic countries.

Not far to the north of Taxco in the mountains of eastern Michoacán, an annual ritual of a very different kind takes place. In November, the monarch butterflies begin to

arrive after completing an awesome migration of thousands of miles from Canada and the northern United States. Eventually they number in the tens of millions, all returning to

half a dozen tiny sanctuaries at an altitude of nearly 10,500 feet. Here they begin their ageless cycle of regeneration. By April they have departed, to repeat once again their

long voyage northward.

Michoacán is a mountainous state and considered by many to be one of the most scenic areas in Mexico. In the Náhuatl language, Michoacán means "place of fisherman," an appropriate description considering this area's numerous lakes. One of the largest is Lake Pátzcuaro, surrounded by volcanoes and the villages of the Tarascan Indians. Today many Indians still venture forth onto the lake with their traditional canoes and butterfly fishing nets, hoping to snare pescado blanco, the lake's famous white fish.

Lake Pátzcuaro settles into dusk as the last rays of the day explode above the island of Janitzio. The Tarascan Indians hold strongly to many of their artistic and social traditions and this is no more apparent than during the Dia de Muertos (Day of the Dead). Although this fiesta is observed throughout Mexico, the celebrations held in the villages near Lake Pátzcuaro are among the country's most colorful.

The Day of the Dead gives expression to the Indians' belief that this is the time when the souls of the deceased return to visit their living relatives. Consequently, these are moments to be anticipated, celebrated, and enjoyed. The markets are full of special holiday foods, flowers, and crafts. Here, two young children buy sugar skulls personalized with their names, reflective of the gentle humor with which Mexicans regard death.

A family offers for sale the crucifixes they have carved and painted, spreading them on a bench in Pátzcuaro's town square. Surrounded by symbols of their faith, they exude a serene and comfortable harmony.

During the final evening of the Day of the Dead the Zapotec Indians of Mitla near Oaxaca participate in a Dance of Death, where spectral apparitions accompanied by young men dressed as beautiful señoritas dance through the streets.

One of the principal obligations of this fiesta is to clean and decorate the graves of family members. Near Cuernavaca, an elderly man, lost in thought, is surrounded by marigolds and carnations that brighten the cemetery in Ocotepec, where the colorfully painted tombs have become works of folk art.

In the Tarascan village of Tzintzuntzán near Pátzcuaro, the most important ritual of the Day of the Dead occurs on the evening of 2 November, when families gather in the cemetery to begin a night-long vigil. The graves are decorated with flowers and lit by hundreds of candles that surround baskets holding a meal of delicacies known to be favored

by the deceased. At six o'clock church bells call "the dead" and incense is burned, its fragrance guiding the spirits to their feast. At dawn everyone returns to their homes, tired but happy, for in having remembered the dead they can freely rejoice in life.

Sixty-two miles west of Lake Pátzcuaro in the volcanic belt of the Sierra Madre Occidental is Paricutín, a barren black cone that startled the world when it blew its top on 24 February 1943. Two Tarascan villages were totally buried in the lava, leaving only a bell tower to mark their existence. Today Paricutín is dormant, taking a siesta. Its ominous summit shrouded in clouds dominates the horizon.

Hundreds of dancers fill the great plaza in front of the basilica, many of them dressed in the elaborate, plumed costumes of Aztec warriors for the "Dance of the Concheros."

Each year more than six million of the faithful visit the Virgin's basilica. Many arrive on 12 December for the fiesta of Our Lady of Guadalupe, where a dancer performs in the "Dance of the Christians and Moors."

THE LEGEND OF OUR LADY OF GUADALUPE

Not long after the Spanish conquest, an Indian, Juan Diego, was walking in the hills near Mexico City when he heard his name called. Looking up, he beheld the Virgin Mary, who told him that she wanted a temple built on the site. When Juan Diego related his experience to the Archbishop, he was dismissed as a simpleton. The following day, Juan Diego was walking in the same area when the Virgin appeared a second time and repeated her request. When he explained the Archbishop's incredulity, the Virgin responded by causing roses in bloom to appear on the bare hilltop. As these flowers had never been seen in Mexico before, this was the miracle that Juan Diego needed to prove his story. He wrapped them in his cloak and went to the Archbishop. This time the clergyman was convinced, for when Juan Diego opened his cape, not only did the roses spill out, but an image of the Virgin appeared on the fabric. That the Virgin should choose a poor Indian to be the vehicle of her miracles greatly endeared her to the indigenous peoples of Mexico. That her skin as it appeared on the cloak was not white but brown also persuaded the Indians that they were her chosen people. Juan Diego's cloak with the image of the Virgin was carried as the banner of liberty during the War of Independence; today it hangs in the basilica of Guadalupe. Except for the Vatican, the basilica of the Virgin of Guadalupe is visited by more people than any other religious site in the Christian world.

Turning his head, an Aztec dancer reveals a golden skeleton on the back of his headdress.

Crowned with golden rays, a masked dancer representing Santiago (St. James) leads the "Dance of the Santiagueros."

Balancing on a tightrope, a dancer performs the "Dance of the Maromeros" with the basilica in the background.

A musician in an elaborate feathered headdress chants while playing a traditional instrument similar to a mandolin.

Hundreds of thousands of pilgrims pour into the great plaza for the fiesta of Our Lady of Guadalupe. Many return home having been entertained, blessed, and then recorded

on film by a local photographer who performs miracles of his own with backdrops, costumes, and props.

A burro is tethered to a giant cactus, its spreading branches providing a shady canopy in the late afternoon heat.

NORTHERN MEXICO

CHIHUAHUA, COAHUILA, DURANGO, NUEVO LEÓN, SONORA, AND TAMAULIPAS

The cornucopia silhouette of Mexico broadens in the north to encompass six of the country's largest states—yet they only hold a fraction of the population. Much of this area is mountainous with the Sierra Madre Occidental paralleling the western coast and the Sierra Madre Oriental along the eastern coast. In between these two ranges sits the Altiplano, an immense plateau with an average altitude of 6,500-8,200 feet. Narrow plains line both coasts.

Mexico's north is so vast (especially in the days when the territory included California and Texas) that its history features many episodes of foiled attempts at colonization. Conquest and development were protracted and painful experiences, made especially so by the indigenous tribes that waged almost continuous war on the colonists, and also by the

tremendous distances and geophysical barriers that separated the settlements. Zacatecas, one of the richest and most elegant of Mexico's great silver mining boomtowns, marked the point where the cultural and economic unity of the heartland gave way to the wilderness of the north.

When settlements did take root, they were of a localized nature, hinging on the fortunes of single cities rather than on regional development. The independent spirit fostered by this fragmentation made it increasingly difficult to accept the rule of a centralized government based in Mexico City. When the 1910 Revolution began, all the leaders of the uprising, except Emiliano Zapata, hailed from the northern states. Today, political opposition to the central government remains strong in the cities of the north.

The Río Bravo (known in the U.S. as the Rio Grande) makes a slow wide bend in its approach to the Sierra Rica Mountains of northern Chihuahua. The thick sediment laid down by the river's passage has rewarded the farmers of this valley with rich harvests for over 1,500 years.

*F*arther east in Coahuila the Río Bravo slashes its way through the towering limestone escarpment of the Sierra del Carmen. Forming the border between Texas and Mexico, the river has cut a series of spectacular canyons within Big Bend National Park. Adjoining Big Bend, the International Park of the Río Bravo is planned by the Mexican government to protect 1.2 million acres of wilderness, including the distinctive ecology of the Sierra del Carmen.

Sixty-two miles west of the capital of Chihuahua and surrounding the town of Cuauhtémoc is an area of great agricultural abundance. At the turn of the century, Mennonite families from Canada were awarded land grants from the Mexican government that permitted them to settle and farm these lands. Originating in Holland during the

Anabaptist movement of the Protestant Reformation, Mennonites had established other communities in Germany, Russia, and America. They have prospered in Mexico, for here they have been able to embrace the newest agricultural methods and simultaneously preserve their religious principles.

Deep in the Sierra Madre a graceful plume of water drops over 820 feet into a pool of perpetual mist. Owing to the immense amphitheater of gigantic cliffs surrounding it, the scale of Basaseachic Falls can be deceptive; it is the highest waterfall in Mexico, and certainly one of the world's most beautiful. After their awesome plunge, the waters of Basaseachic pass through the vertiginous ravine of Barranca de Candamena, where they mingle with the waters from five other equally spectacular cascades to create one of North America's most impressive canyon landscapes.

The rugged mountains of the western Sierra Madre divide the high plains of central Mexico from the coastal lowlands. For nearly 1,000 miles, from the U.S. border south to Guadalajara, only four roads cross this formidable barrier. In southern Chihuahua, the Cañon del Cobre (Copper Canyon) carves its tortuous way through the Sierra. The pale green waters of the Río Urique ripple between daggers of rock as it enters the Cañon del Cobre near Humira.

Below the overlook at Divisadero, the Río Urique turns abruptly south and enters the deepest segment of the canyon. The famous Chihuahua-Pacific railroad reaches the canyon

rim at this point and continues westward through eighty-eight tunnels and across thirty-eight bridges before reaching Los Mochis on the Pacific coastal plain. Work on the line

was begun at the end of the last century and only after overcoming enormous engineering difficulties was it finally completed in 1961.

The sun's last rays paint the clouds crimson above the rim of Cañon del Cobre at Divisadero. At 7,500 feet, it is the deepest canyon in North America, half again as deep as the Grand Canyon.

Although this remote mountainous area may appear uninhabited, it is in fact home to more than 50,000 Tarahumara Indians. Where they once lived on canyon rims, the Indians over the last centuries have been displaced, and now eke out a basic existence in the canyon's less inaccessible areas. The Tarahumara call themselves Raramuri, which translates as "the foot runners." They are renowned for their prodigious ability to run nonstop, sometimes for days at a time, through this near-vertical terrain. Today the Tarahumara continue their marathon running ways even though their canyons have been invaded by four-wheel-drive pickups and mountain bikes.

In the northwestern corner of Sonora, above the Gulf of California, is the heart of the Sonoran Desert. The Pinacate Grand Desert National Park is a stark landscape of volcanic craters and baked and blackened lava fields, punctuated by spectacular desert flora: giant saguaro, ocotillo, and cholla cacti.

Prickly pear cacti, their petals fringed with deep red fruit, ring many small villages in the state of Durango. The plants grow up to ten feet tall, and when planted in hedges, create both natural corrals for farm animals and an easily harvested food source.

From beneath her parasol, a shy young girl flashes a smile as bright as the desert sun.

*T*he sea horse statue has graced the malecón *(Puerto Vallarta's seafront promenade)* for so many years that it has become the symbol of the city. Nearby are the restaurants, shops, and nightlife of Puerto Vallarta.

PACIFIC COAST

Born of the inexorable push and pull of tectonic plates, a folded mass of mountain ranges—literally the spine of Mexico—stretches over 2,480 miles from the California border south to Guatemala. In many places these mountains hug the coast, their slopes dropping steeply into the sea. At other points, narrow coastal plains separate the mountains from the ocean. Much of this fertile flatland is dedicated to large-scale agricultural endeavors (harvests include sugarcane, fruit, and vegetables), the bulk of it destined to travel north to American tables. In return, millions of tourists head south to play along Mexico's golden beaches at Puerto Vallarta, Acapulco, Mazatlán, Ixtapa, and the Bahías de Huatulco.

The great resorts are relatively small enclaves on this lengthy coastline, interspersed between vast expanses of undeveloped beaches, tropical lagoons, and rocky headlands. A diverse climate creates a distinctive character for each region. In the north, the Sonoran Desert sweeps the coast with a dry, rocky landscape dotted with giant saguaro, its shores gently lapped by the torpid waters of the Gulf of California (Sea of Cortés). Below Mazatlán, the coast is exposed to the more violent weather patterns of the Pacific; desert landscapes give way to temperate climes that are in turn supplanted by humid tropical jungles along the southernmost stretches.

*M*oments after the sun drops into the Pacific, Acapulco's near-perfect harbor turns burnished red, the lights of its hotels and villas circling it like a necklace of pearls; appropriate for

a city that has been called the Pearl of the Pacific. Pearls were among the precious commodities of the Orient that arrived here in the "black ships," the Spanish galleons of the

sixteenth and seventeenth centuries. From 1530, Acapulco was the only harbor open to the fleets from China and the Philippines; this monopoly brought great prosperity, as well as the attention of Dutch and English pirates.

The coast is fringed with bays, estuaries, and lagoons, with salt marshes and mangrove swamps providing breeding grounds for a profusion of wildlife. The Coyuca lagoon north of Acapulco is three times the size of the famous bay. Separated from the sea by an eleven-mile sandbar, its protective waters are a sanctuary for water hyacinth, herons, and egrets.

North of Acapulco, along the costa de Michoacán, the Sierra Madre del Sur tumbles abruptly into the sea. For 125 miles the coast highway winds precipitously around cliffs hundreds of feet above the pounding surf. A chain of idyllic beaches mark where rivers have successfully carved their passage through the mountains to meet the sea. Here, two fishermen wade upstream through a tunnel of lush tropical vegetation.

Continuing northward, the rugged Michoacán shore finally gives way to the gentler slopes of Colima. South of Manzanillo Bay is the lovely Laguna de Cuyutlán, its waters an unruffled iridescence at sunrise. A fisherman in a dugout canoe prepares his nets, while pelicans, herons, and cranes fly overhead or observe from their perches on a fish trap.

Inland from Laguna de Cuyutlán the terrain climbs steadily toward Volcán de Fuego (12,530 feet) in the foreground and Volcán de Colima (13,907 feet) behind. Fuego is one of the most active volcanoes in Mexico and forms the western boundary of the Sierra Volcánica, a broad band of volcanoes that crosses the country eastward toward Veracruz and contains Mexico's highest peaks. The ash from countless eruptions has made the area around Volcán de Fuego ideal for orchards and fields of sugarcane.

*S*ix *miles south of Puerto Vallarta is the beautiful beach of Mismaloya, made famous in John Huston's film* The Night of the Iguana, *starring Richard Burton and Ava Gardner. A few miles inland is a true paradise called Edén de Mismaloya, where a small cascade tumbles over boulders in the midst of impenetrable jungle growth. This site, too, made note in the cinematic textbooks as the location for Arnold Schwarzenegger's* Predator.

When Huston's film crew arrived in the sleepy fishing village of Puerto Vallarta, it was quite an exciting event—but when Richard Burton and Elizabeth Taylor chose to make their vacation home here, it caused a sensation and put Puerto Vallarta on the map. Today dozens of posh resorts line the coast, but elements of the old town remain, such as the church of Guadalupe, where on special occasions the beautiful crown, which tops its bell tower, is lit.

A *fisherman casts his net into the Mexcaltitán lagoon near San Blas. Mexcaltitán is a curious town built on a small island in the lagoon and nicknamed the Venice of Mexico because all local transportation is by canoe. Some historians believe it might have been the original home of the Aztecs because of similarities in the construction of Mexcaltitán and the Aztec capital of Tenochtitlán.*

At Los Mochis the mountains retreat from the sea, leaving an expansive coastal plain that has become prime agricultural land. The city was founded in 1872 by a young American engineer who saw the potential for sugarcane cultivation. He was also one of the first to envision a railroad linking the Pacific and Chihuahua via the Cañon del Cobre, a dream that was realized almost 100 years later.

Sited on a rocky promontory that projects into the blue waters of the Gulf of California (Sea of Cortés), Guaymas is the main port of Sonora and boasts one of the largest fishing fleets on Mexico's Pacific coast.

Baja Peninsula

Baja California and Baja California Sur

Notwithstanding the explosion of mega-resorts on its southern coasts and *maquiladores* (multinational companies) along its northern border, Baja California remains Mexico's final frontier. Located west of Mexico's vast, northern territories, the peninsula has always been underpopulated and barely explored. In 1683, Father Francisco Kino, a Jesuit missionary who had great success in Sonora and Arizona, attempted to establish a mission in Baja. He was unsuccessful, closed the colony shortly thereafter and left to pursue his missionary work in northern Mexico. Even the aboriginal Indians that Father Kino was seeking to convert did not flourish; of the 40,000 original inhabitants, only a few hundred remain.

What has flourished is Baja's bizarre and wondrous flora. As in Lewis Carroll's *Through the Looking Glass,* the deeper travelers venture into the interior, the "curiouser and curiouser" the landscape becomes. The magnificent cardón, the world's tallest cactus; whip-like ocotillo; fuzzy cholla; and elephant trees, with their gnarled and peeling trunks, decorate the landscape. The strangest of all is the boojum tree, so named in another reference to the fantasy world of Lewis Carroll's *The Hunting of the Snark.* Some liken the boojum to an inverted carrot; the Spanish, however, thought of it as a tall, tapering candle and consequently called it *cirio* (candle).

The peninsula's fauna is equally fascinating. From offshore islands, elephant seals and Guadalupe fur seals watch the pods of huge gray whales arrive in January on their annual migration. The whales mate and calve in the shallow lagoons along Baja's west coast. By June they have departed on their 6,000-mile return journey to the colder, nutrient-rich waters of the north.

Baja has been inhabited for a very long time, possibly well before the rest of Mexico. Groups of Paleolithic hunter-gatherers passing from Asia down the coast of North America found their way onto the peninsula about 7,000 years ago. The most intriguing artifacts that remain of their culture are numerous rock art sites that date between A.D. 500 and 1500.

The Spanish first explored the coast of Baja in 1532, but it was 1697 before the first of twenty missions was successfully founded by the Jesuits. Then came Mexican colonizers, followed by English and Russian agriculturists, who established farms and vineyards in the north; French miners who worked copper from the hills of Santa Rosalía on the Gulf coast; Chinese laborers who settled around Mexicali; sailors speaking a myriad of languages berthed in

Tourists aren't the only sun-worshippers in Baja. Here, three of the locals perch on a cardón and soak up the morning sunlight.

Baja's ports; and most recently North Americans, many who came first as tourists but returned to become residents. Because of this vital mix of heritages, Baja, more than any other area of Mexico, is infused with a multicultural spirit and identity where the frontier virtues of hard work and rugged independence remain.

At dawn the Gulf of California (Sea of Cortés), south of Loreto, is aglow. Loreto was the first European settlement in the Californias and served as its capital for 132 years. After devastation by a hurricane in 1829, Loreto was abandoned in favor of a new capital, La Paz. Thanks to a proliferation of game fish, Loreto is back on the map, this time as the ultimate destination for anglers.

The completion of the 1,054-mile Transpeninsular Highway in 1973 made many isolated parts of the Baja accessible for the first time. Today the road runs through the splendid desert scenery of the Cataviña Boulderfield and has made possible the creation of the surrounding Parque Natural del Desierto Central.

The forms of giant cardón cactus, graceful elephant trees, and whimsical boojum trees are silhouetted at dusk in the Cataviña Boulderfield. Nowhere else is the peninsula's exotic flora in more extraordinary evidence.

Although hundreds of rock art sites have been discovered, the paintings at Cueva Pintada in Arroyo de San Pablo are considered to be the most magnificent examples. Here, a series of figures, some more than thirty feet tall, decorate a gallery that extends for 525 feet along the canyon wall. Men and women with upraised arms are seen amidst a herd of running deer, while birds and mountain sheep look on.

From a distance the Sierras San Francisco and San Juan seem isolated and foreboding; however, with perseverance and a surefooted burro, they yield small oases found deep within hidden canyons.

Cueva Flecha is so named because of the arrows (flechas) that pierce the painted figures here. The meaning is unknown: Does the scene depict an invasion or a civil war, some cataclysmic battle that drove these artists from their homes five hundred years ago?

At the bottom of Arroyo de San Pablo in the Sierra San Francisco, graceful palms rise tall above tranquil spring-fed pools. The canyon's murals bear witness to an ancient way of life with paintings of people, animals, birds, and even whales remaining as a record of the Paleolithic tribes that lived here for a thousand years.

Star trails streak the desert sky above a giant cardón cactus and an elephant tree in the Cataviña Boulderfield in north-central Baja. The skyline is illuminated by the rising full moon, made bright in this three-hour time exposure.

The old Camino Real meanders toward the jagged peaks of the Sierra de la Giganta, possibly the most rugged part of the peninsula. The royal highway carried Spanish missionaries and explorers between San Javier Mission (founded in 1699) and the coastal town of Loreto.

In contrast to the arid landscapes of Baja California Sur are the verdant fields of the Valle de Mexicali irrigated by the waters of the Colorado River. As if to emphasize man's role in creating this fertile agricultural area, the giant Algodones Dunes loom on the horizon, ever present reminders that by nature this is one of the driest regions of North America.

Finisterra, Land's End, and El Arco are all references to the rocky outcrop that is the southernmost tip of the Baja Peninsula. The booming resort of Cabo San Lucas meets the bay just beyond the foreground cliffs. Near the arch suntanned visitors frolic on Playa del Amor to the amusement of the sea lions lounging on the surrounding rocks.